Non Sequitur's
Beastly Things

Also by Wiley

The Non Sequitur Survival Guide for the Nineties

Non Sequitur's Beastly Things

By WILEY

Introduction by Jules Feiffer

Andrews McMeel
Publishing

Kansas City

First, a word from the legal department . . .

www.andrewsmcmeel.com

99 00 01 02 03 BAH 10 9 8 7 6 5 4 3 2 1

ISBN: 0-7407-0016-2

Library of Congress Catalog Card Number: 99-72691

ATTENTION: SCHOOLS AND BUSINESSES

Andrews McMeel books are available at quantity discounts with bulk purchase for educational, business, or sales promotional use. For information, write: Special Sales Department, Andrews McMeel Publishing, 4520 Main Street, Kansas City, Missouri 64111.

GO AHEAD, INFRINGE ON THE COPYRIGHT.

MAKE MY DAY...

NIT WRIT

Duncan, Harpo, Monty,
and Mack.

Table of Contents

Introduction

What other cartoonist is sly enough to figure out a style to fit his name?

Wily, as in tricky, as in clever, as in canny, as in deceptive—and, oh yes, the not-to-be-forgotten foxy.

Wiley, as in while you, the reader, can't figure out the cartoonist, he, the cartoonist, has got the goods on you: He knows when you are sleeping, he knows when you're awake, he knows when you are bad or good—and he knows, what's more, that you are never good, that good is a cover-up for something else, that *everything* is a cover-up for something else, that humanity is a cover-up for stupidity.

And while Wiley chooses, thank God, to ignore our major stupidities, he is an indefatigable chronicler of the small, mind-numbing, niggling stupidities that set off our days, moment by barely bearable moment.

Wiley has taken the form introduced by Hap Kliban and popularized by Gary Larson. He's removed its *Far Side* cutes and added bite. His visual puns differ from Larson's whimsy. Wiley's whimsy is darker, more sardonic, less Dada and gaga, more theater of the absurd.

He looks down on life, but as you can tell from his drawings, it's only from the second floor. A bird's-eye view—modified. No eagle eye here; he's perched too close for that—more of a pigeon's eye. He sees from this closest of distances how small we are, how little we strive for, how great the divide is between us and them. Anyone who is not us is a "them." Lawyers. Doctors. Husbands. Wives. The Other. Them.

"Them" are not to be trusted. Often enough, "them" are not even to be noticed. "Them" are ridiculous in ways we could never be, until, a few pages later—wait a minute!—we are "them."

There is an *Invasion of the Body Snatchers* quality to Wiley's work. These alien forms are in the process of taking us over—until there is no "us" left. To paraphrase Walt Kelly, we have met "us," and we are "them."

Read it and you will laugh, and you will groan, and you will cry foul.

Jules Feiffer
February 1999

The foundation of all art, science, and society – indeed our very existence – is our relationship to one another.

Which probably explains why deserted islands are so universally appealing...

Relationships

16

EMPLOYING HIS PERSONAL-ENERGY-CONSERVATION-THEORY, BILL ATTEMPTS TO SKEW THE AVERAGE LIFESPAN STATISTICS BY LIVING FOREVER

MORT'S SUSPICION OF HIS STATURE IN THE COMMUNITY IS CONFIRMED...

17

WORST CASE SCENARIO OF PERSONAL ASSESSMENT

PARK

I AM NOT INVISIBLE

WHY RHETORICAL QUESTIONS AND MARRIAGE DON'T MIX...

OF COURSE I DON'T THINK YOU'RE A HAS-BEEN, DEAR. YOU NEED TO HAVE *BEEN* SOMETHING FIRST BEFORE YOU CAN BE A HAS-BEEN...

COURTSHIP IN THE NINETIES

29

ENVIRONMENTAL
NO-FAULT DIVORCE

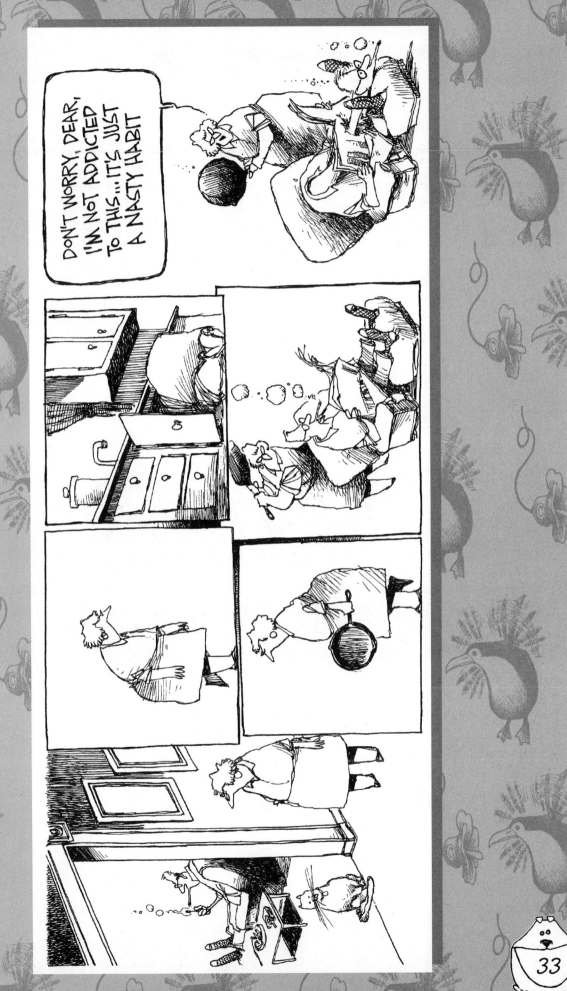

33

35

With the Hippocratic Oath today being a distant second to the Bottom Line, the once proud medical profession now takes its place alongside the legal profession in public esteem, thus insuring an unending source of material for smart-ass cartoonists.

45

The Examination Room

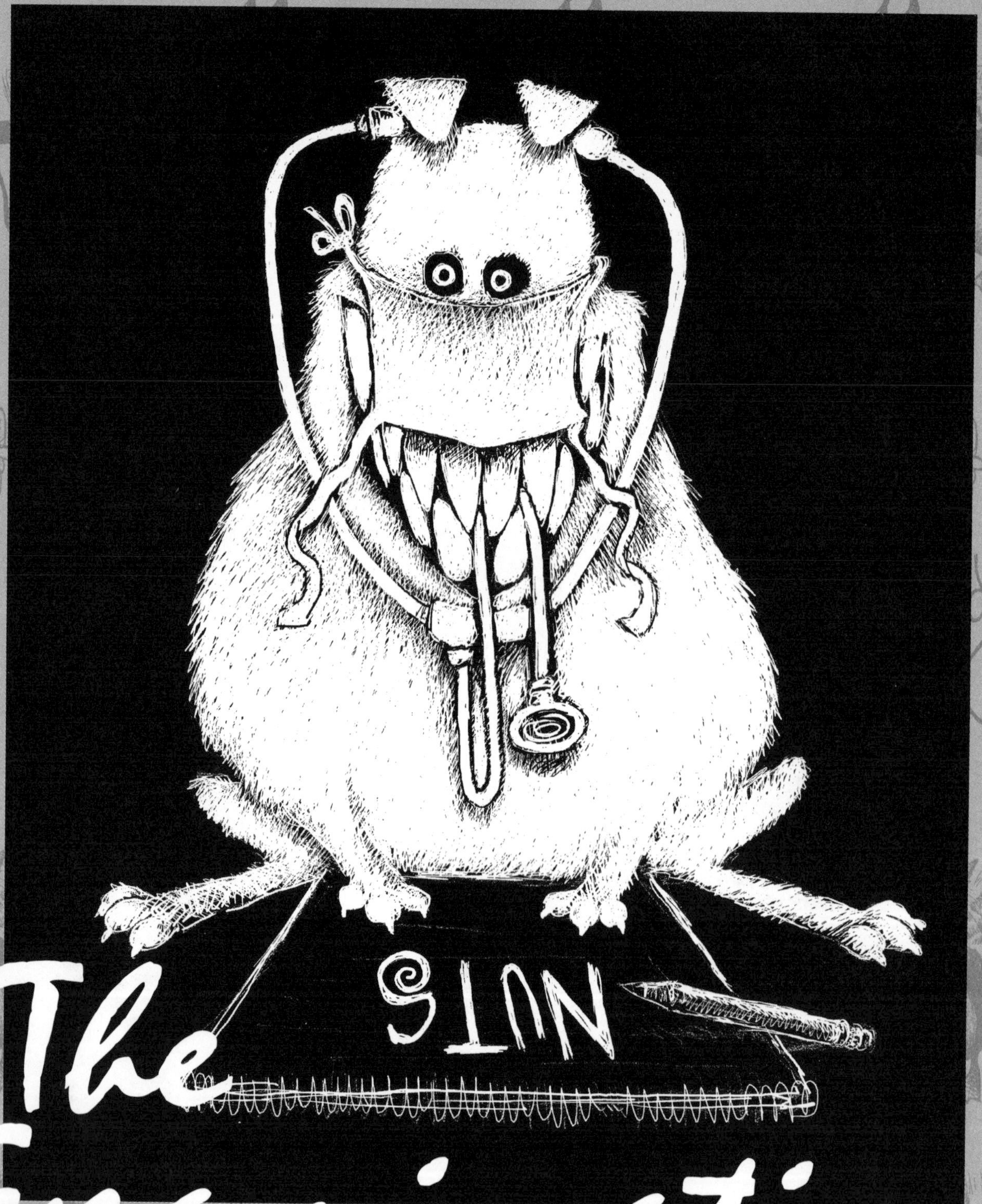

NUTS

47

49

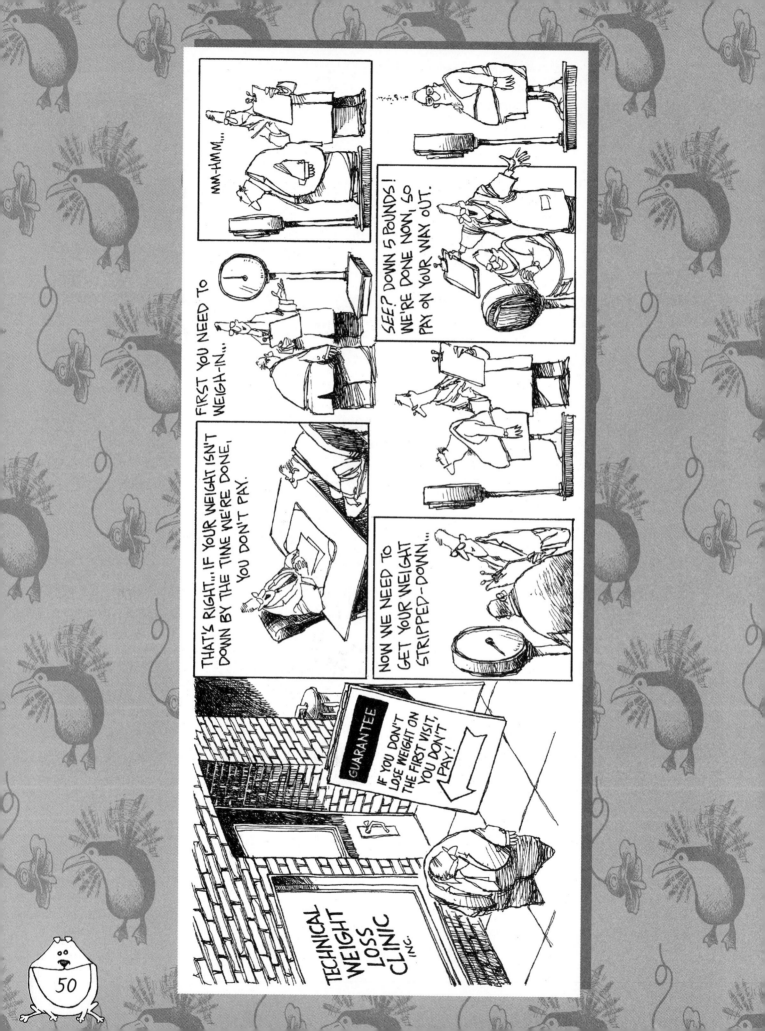

50

53

ARNIE'S EPIPHANY ABOUT AMERICAN WEIGHT CONSCIOUSNESS.

THE FIRST STOP IN THE TOBACCO EXECUTIVES' SEARCH FOR A NEW SPOKESMAN...

WHY MEN'S GROUP THERAPY SESSIONS TAKE SO LONG...

OK...THE SECOND QUARTER HAS STARTED, SO WE'LL GET BACK TO LARRY'S FEELINGS ABOUT BEING IGNORED DURING HALFTIME

They don't call it
the Bored Room
for nothin'...

Basic Business

HOW TO TELL WHEN WE'VE BECOME ACCUSTOMED TO STOCK MARKET CRASHES...

ALBERT WILL ATTEMPT A TRIPLE-AXEL, REVERSE JACK KNIFE FROM THE PIKE POSITION, WHICH HAS A DEGREE OF DIFFICULTY OF TEN STORIES

INTRODUCING OVERBOOKED-MY-BUTT! I'VE-GOT-TO-BE-ON-THAT-FLIGHT CLASS

GENERIC AIRLINES

THE GOOD NEWS WAS, JIM CONFIRMED THAT HE WASN'T BEING PARANOID...

TYPE 'A' CORP.

SO WHAT HAVE YOU DONE FOR US LATELY?

61

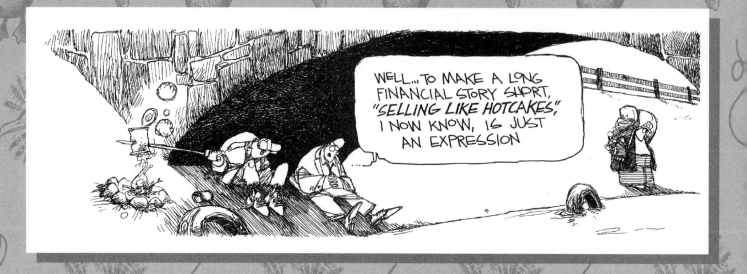

64

MODERN MEASUREMENT OF CORPORATE PRODUCTIVITY...

IN   OUT   LAW SUITS

THE CAPTAIN HAS TURNED ON THE NO-WHINING SIGN...

WHEN AIRLINES SHOW THEIR GENUINE CONCERN ABOUT FLIGHT DELAYS

67

WHEN TEMPS
TURN PRO

81

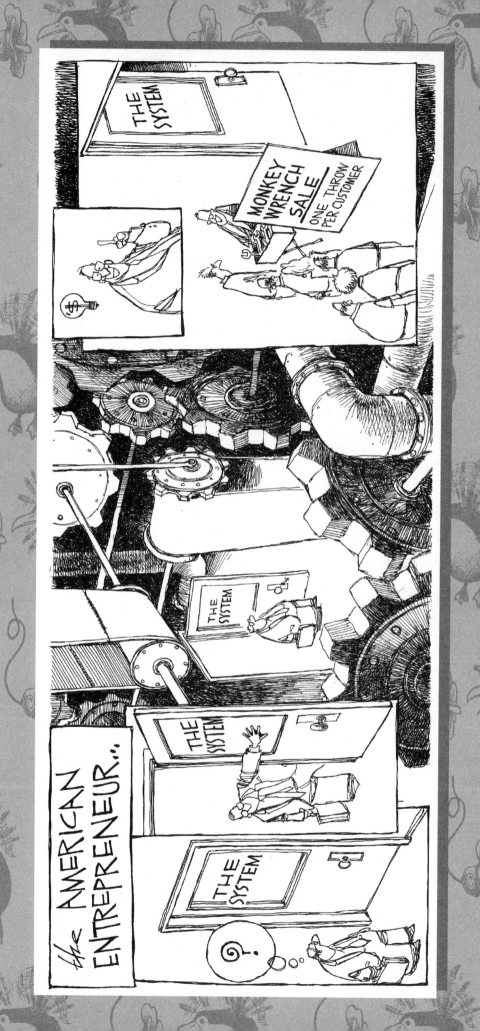

85

ALAN DECIDES TO BUCK THE WORK-AT-HOME TREND AND KEEP COMMUTING

WHEN YOUR CREDIT LINE GETS PERMANENTLY ESTABLISHED...

CREDIT BUREAU

TODAY'S TARGET FOR FINANCIAL HELL

87

89

93

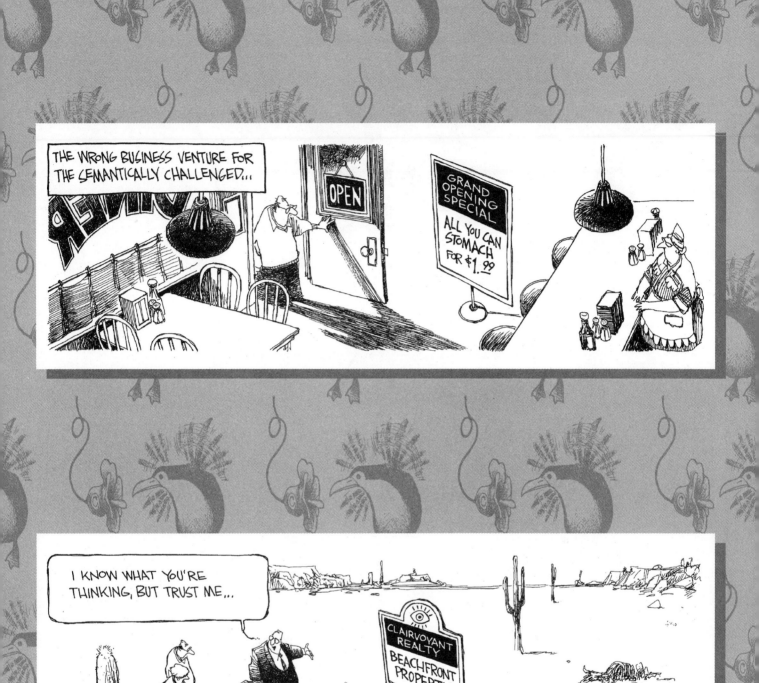

96

It has been said that
"American Culture"
is an oxymoron.

Speaking on behalf of
satirists everywhere,
thank God!

97

Real

Culture

105

THE GAUNTLET...

107

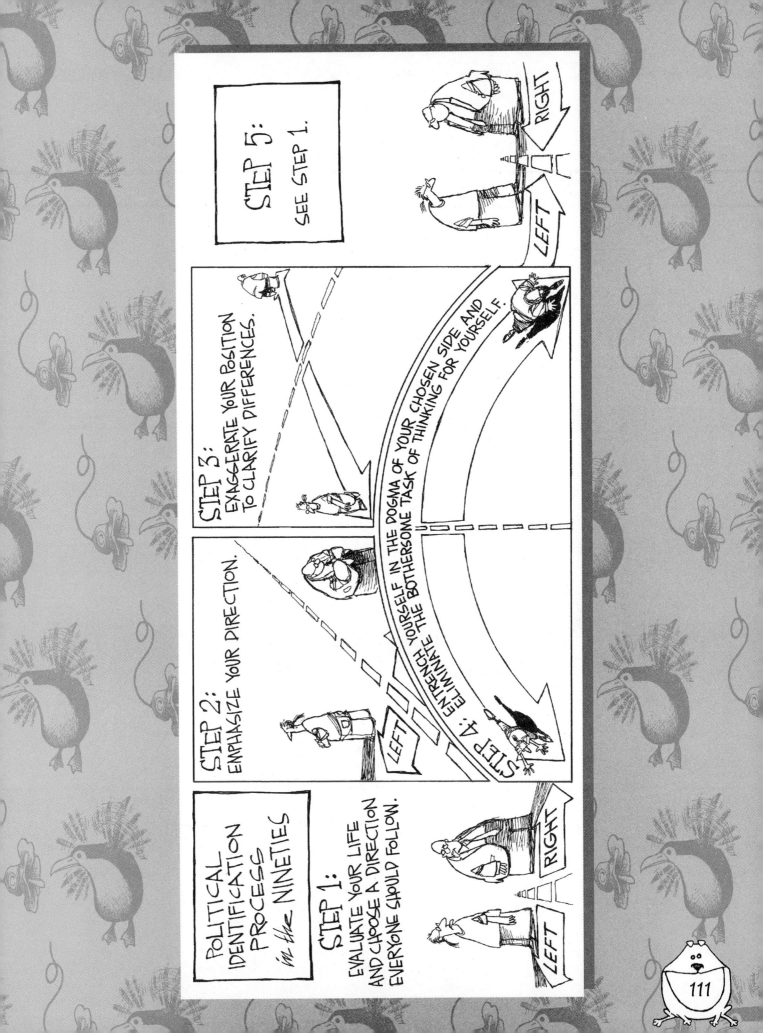

LENNY'S CONVERSION TO LONG HAIR AND VEGETARIANISM...

SAFETY PATROL in the NINETIES...

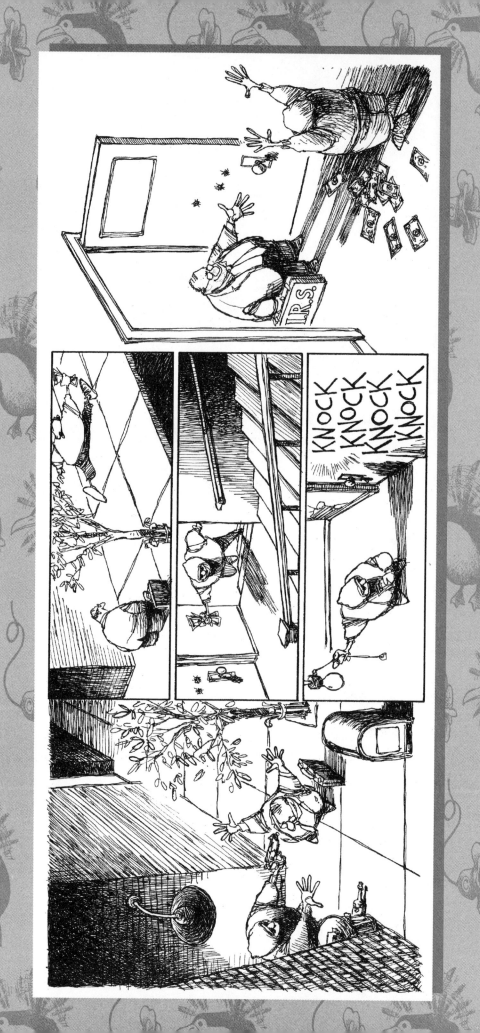

116

119

WHEN MEN
TURN FIFTY

WHEN THE LAST PROPONENT OF URBAN LIVING DECIDES TO MOVE OUT OF THE CITY...

U.S. DEPARTMENT of PRECISE MEASUREME...

THE WAY WE SHOULD BE VERSUS HUMAN NATURE

DELIVERIES HEALTH FOOD ONLY

GOOD FOR YOU CAFE

TO HELL WITH IT GRILL

HEALTHFUL LOW FAT FOOD OPEN

STUFF YOU KNOW IS REALLY BAD FOR YOU OPEN

ESCAPE IN THE NINETIES...

STATE PENITENTIARY

133

THE TROUBLE WITH PUBLIC BEACHES...

WHEN POLITICAL CORRECTNESS BECOMES MAINSTREAM...

THE NEW YORK CITY WALK OF FAME

Corleone's FAMILY RESTAURANT

ONCE AGAIN, DAVE REMEMBERS WHY HE HATES HIGH SCHOOL REUNIONS...

TRUST ME... YOU'RE NOT REGISTERED ON THIS LIST

WELCOME BAC CLASS of '69

LANGLEY H.S. 25 YEAR REUNION

COOL GUYS, JOCKS AND CHEER-LEADERS

REGISTRATION DESK

DWEEBS

GEEKS

OTHER

HERE BUT FOR THE GRACE OF GOD GO YOU

THE KING of GUILT AND HIS SUBJECTS

EARLY MAN *in* EARLY FALL...

SUMMER WARDROBE

WINTER WARDROBE

THE MANTRA of the NINETIES...

I'M A VICTIM OF

YOUR FAVORITE NEUROSIS PRINTED HERE

146

147

THE NEW FAVORITE AMERICAN PASTIME...

...AND IT'S TAILS. THE HOME TEAM ELECTS TO RECEIVE THE KICKOFF, AND THE VISITORS CHOOSE TO FILE A MOTION IN DISTRICT COURT

WELL, IF YOU ASK ME, I THINK THEY'RE TRYING *TOO* HARD TO MAKE TRAIN TRAVEL MORE EXCITING...

ESPRESSO $1.00

WHEN LESTER GAVE UP TRYING TO FIGURE OUT THE NINETIES...

THE BOOK STORE

COFFEE CAFE

TODAY'S SPECIAL
· LATTE
· ESPRESSO
· FRENCH ROAST

TODAY'S SPECIAL
· SUSAN MINOT
· DAVID LEAVITT
· DONNA TARTT
· M. CHABON

152

POLITICAL SCIENCE IN THE NINETIES...

101

1. DEMAND TOLERANCE OF YOUR POINT OF VIEW.
2. GIVE NONE TO OTHERS.

CLASS DISMISSED

AT THE *VERY* FRENCH REVOLUTION...

PLEASE WAIT TO BE HEADED

THE MOST EMBARRASSING DEFEAT IN BARBARIAN HISTORY

MUST BE AT LEAST THIS TALL

TO STORM CASTLE

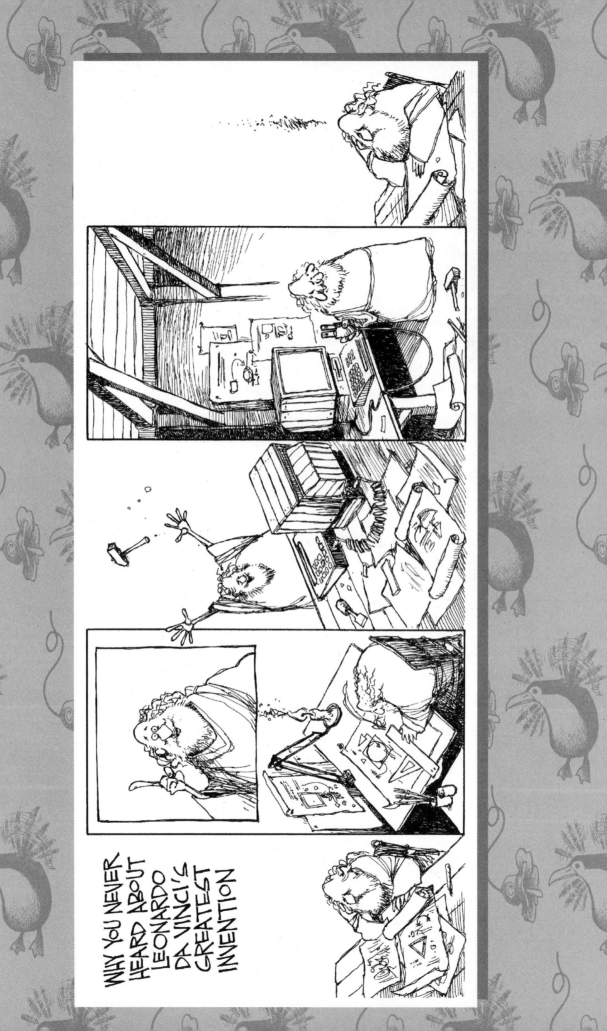

the BACK-TO-BASICS EXERCISE AND DIET PROGRAM...

LOCAL   OUT OF TOWN   WAY OUT OF TOWN

HOW TO TELL IT'S *DEFINITELY* TIME TO LEAVE THE CITY...

157

Holidays and religion.

The great American tradition of
finding an excuse to take another
day off work in order to mock
and ridicule other faiths...

Holy Strokes

THE BIRTH OF A HOLIDAY CLASSIC...

HOW MANY TIMES DO I HAVE TO TELL YOU? IT'S *OVER* THE RIVER AND *THROUGH* THE WOODS...

LAST-MINUTE CHRISTMAS SHOPPING *in the* CITY...

AND ALL THROUGH THE APARTMENT, NOT A CREATURE WAS STIRRING, NOT EVEN A

TWAS THE NIGHT BEFORE CHRISTMAS

164

165

NOT-SO-GOOD FRIDAY...

THE IRONY IS, POLITICAL CORRECTNESS HAS MADE THIS HOLIDAY SCARIER THAN EVER

THE ORIGIN OF THE ANNUAL THANKSGIVING ARGUMENT...

...AND, LAST BUT NOT LEAST, I WANT TO GIVE THANKS THAT FOOTBALL HASN'T BEEN INVENTED YET

167

168

REMEMBER A COUPLE OF MONTHS AGO WHEN WE THOUGHT IT WAS WONDERFUL NEWS THAT THE ACCOUNTANTS STEPPED IN AND SAVED THE THANKSGIVING DAY PARADE...?

WHY THERE ARE ONLY TEN COMMANDMENTS...

THANKS, BUT I CAN'T WAIT FOR ANOTHER TABLET

XI THOU SHALT BE PATIENT
XII

THE CULT VOTED MOST LIKELY TO SUCCEED...

THE WORLD MIGHT END TOMORROW ...SO LIGHTEN UP!

NEWS

THE FIRST INSIDE TRADER...

ARK REALTY SPECIALIZING IN FUTURE OCEANFRONT PROPERTY

NOAH

171

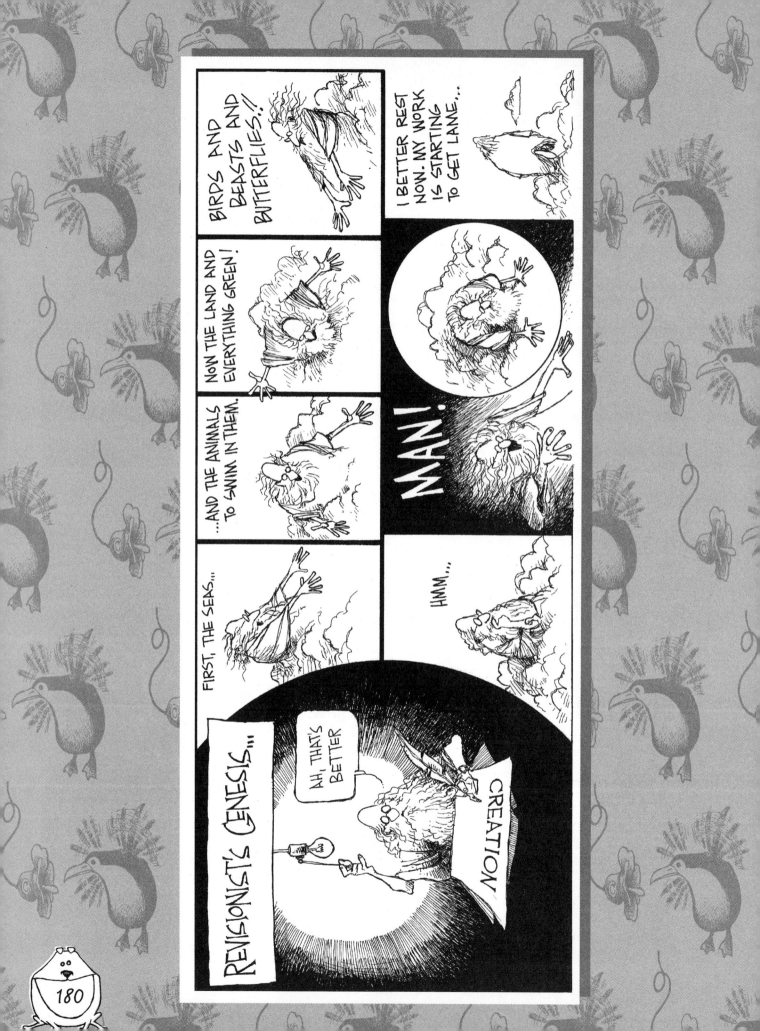

180

181

Arts and Media.

Going together through the ages
like bread and water.

To see for yourself how
well this works, go put a
slice of bread into a
bowl of water...

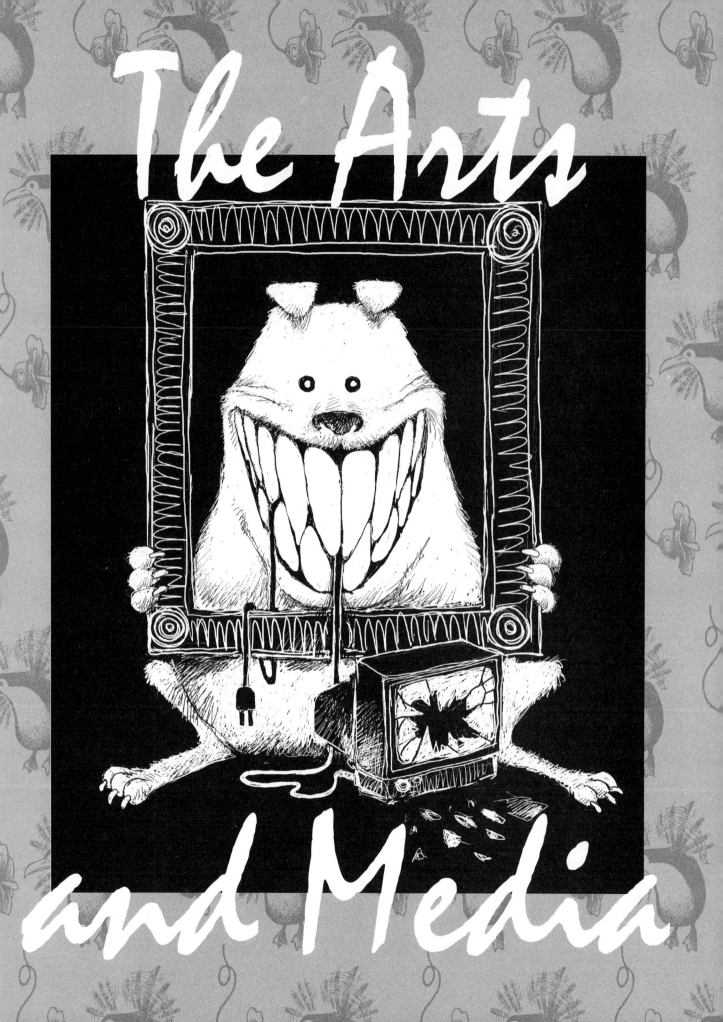

The Arts

and Media

WHEN TV TALK SHOW HOSTS BRING THEIR WORK HOME

189

HOW TO TELL THE MEDIA'S ANNUAL-HOLIDAY-
HUMAN-INTEREST-STORY SEASON HAS BEGUN...

AS SEEN ON TV

AMERICAN CELEBRITY
CONTRACT NEGOTIATIONS...

...AND SINCE THE MEDIA PUTS YOU *UP* ON A PEDESTAL, THEY RESERVE THE OPTION TO KNOCK YOU *OFF* IT.

IT'S STANDARD, AND, IRONICALLY, WHY YOU'RE IN LINE TO TAKE OVER TED DANSON'S SPOT

195

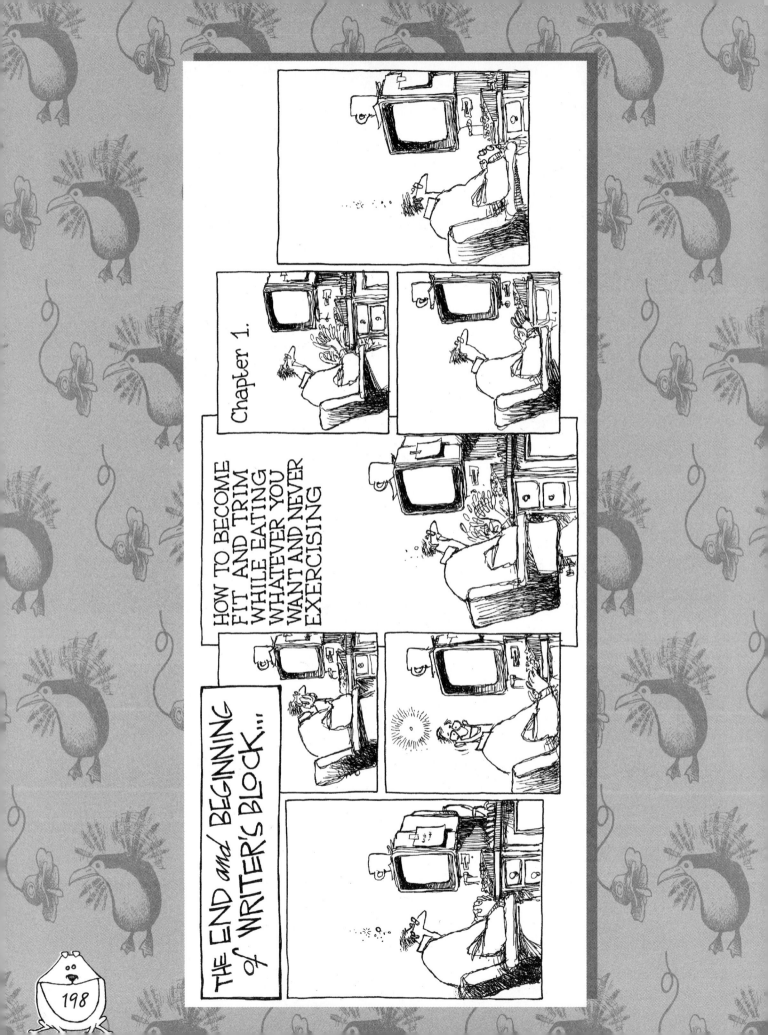

THE SOON-TO-BE RATINGS LEADER

WMOB
HOME of the "HITS"

WMOB RADIO
LISTEN OR ELSE

SPORTS DESK   CITY DESK   ENTERTAINMENT DESK

201

203

HOW TO TELL YOU SHOULD HAVE PAID MORE ATTENTION TO THE REVIEWS OF THE PLAY...

SPIT-WADS 50¢

OFFICIALLY, I'M REALLY PEEVED. PERSONALLY, I WANT HIS AGENT TO NEGOTIATE MY CONTRACTS FROM NOW ON...

TAN LOT

214

MIRIAM'S PLUNGE INTO MINIMALISM

I'VE DECIDED TO ELIMINATE ALL OF MY NON-ESSENTIAL POSSESSIONS.

GOODBYE, HAROLD.

TALK SHOW HOST IN HELL...

...OUR THANKS AGAIN TO MADONNA, HOWARD STERN, AND RUSH LIMBAUGH FOR JOINING US TONIGHT. OUR GUESTS TOMORROW NIGHT, AND FOR THE REST OF ETERNITY, WILL, OF COURSE, BE MADONNA, HOWARD STERN, AND RUSH LIMBAUGH...

Seeing themselves as graced,
human society has
successfully separated itself
from the rest of the
animal kingdom.

For this the animal kingdom
is eternally grateful...

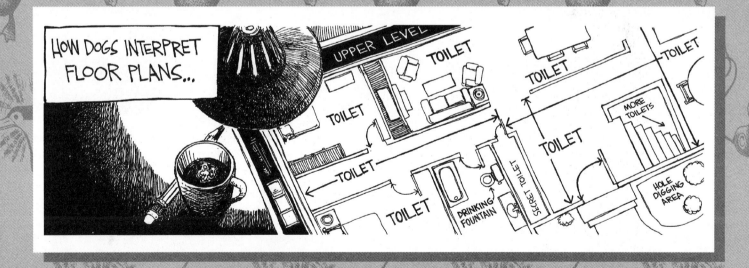

224

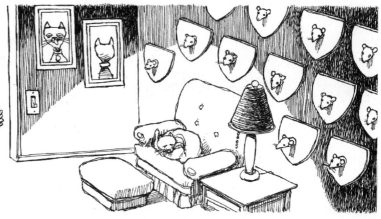

229

"Why do you pick on lawyers?"

A frequent question, not coincidentally, asked only by lawyers.

So in the great legal tradition of giving obtuse answers to direct questions, a response...

According to the Post Office, there are approximately 730,000 postal employees.

According to the American Bar Association, there will be one million attorneys practicing in the United States at the turn of the century.

Do the math folks.

Besides, big targets are easier to hit...

Legal Briefs

238

ALL-AMERICAN JURISPRUDENCE...

...AND, IF AFTER WEIGHING THE EVIDENCE YOU *STILL* FIND MY CLIENT GUILTY, THE BIDDING FOR THE MOVIE RIGHTS WILL BEGIN IMMEDIATELY

A NINETIES HALLOWEEN

TRICK OR TREAT OR LITIGATION

THE SUPREME COURT'S FIRST RULING...

YES, THE FIRST AMENDMENT GUARANTEES FREEDOM OF SPEECH, AND, NO, IT DOESN'T APPLY TO MARRIAGE

SEE?

242

243

THE AMERICAN PRINCIPLE OF PRESUMED IGNORANT UNTIL PROVEN GREEDY

FOR MORE INFORMATION, CALL MY AGENT AND MAKE AN OFFER

MODERN MUGGING...

GIVE OR I'LL SUE

...BECAUSE IT'S CHEAPER THAN DEFENDING MYSELF IN COURT, THAT'S WHY

JURISPRUDENCE in the NINETIES...

YES, YOUR HONOR, WE HAVE REACHED A VERDICT. BUT FIRST, LET'S PAUSE FOR STATION IDENTIFICATION...

IOWA